Literacy Activity Book

Year 1 Term 3

Louis Fidge

EDUCATIONAL

Every effort has been made to trace copyright holders and to obtain their permission for the use of copyright material. The authors and publishers would gladly receive information enabling them to rectify any error or omission in subsequent editions.

Acknowledgements
In The Park by Lucy Coats, taken from *First Rhymes* by Lucy Coats, first published in the UK by Orchard Books in 1994, a division of The Watts Publishing Group Limited, 96 Leonard Street, London EC2A 4XD.

Shoes by John Foster, © 1991 John Foster, first published in *Clothes Poems* (OUP). Reprinted by permission of the author.

First published 2000

Letts Educational
9–15 Aldine Street, London W12 8AW
Tel: 020 8740 2270   Fax: 020 8740 2280

Text © Louis Fidge

Designed by Gecko Limited, Bicester, Oxon
Produced by Ken Vail Graphic Design, Cambridge

Colour reproduction by PDQ, Bungay, Suffolk

Illustrated by Phil Burrows, Rob Englebright, Graham-Cameron Illustration (Tamsin Cook, Bridget Dowty and Kirsty Wilson), Simon Girling & Associates (Mimi Everett and Piers Harper) and Tim Oliver.

British Library Cataloguing-in-Publication Data
A CIP record for this book is available from the British Library

ISBN 1 84085 449 9

Printed in Spain by Mateu Cromo

Letts Educational, a division of Granada Learning Ltd. Part of the Granada Media Group.

Introduction

The Year 1 Literacy Textbooks:

- support the teaching of the Literacy Hour
- are best used along with the *Year 1 Poster Packs* and *Teacher's Notes* which provide more detailed suggestions for development activities
- help meet the majority of the objectives of the National Literacy Strategy Framework (when used in conjunction with the *Year 1 Poster Pack* and *Teacher's Notes*)
- are divided into three books, each containing one term's work
- contain ten units per term (equivalent to one unit a week)
- contain one Writing Focus unit each term to support compositional writing
- provide coverage of a wide range of writing, both fiction and non-fiction, as identified in the National Literacy Strategy Framework
- assume an adult (a teacher, parent or classroom assistant) will be supporting the children, reading to and with them, and mediating the tasks
- assume much of the work will be done orally, with written responses expected only as and when pupils have sufficient competence to record them.

Unit number →

Text for reading and discussion →

Key teaching points →

Text Level activities (purple)

Sentence Level activities (yellow)

Word Level activities (green)

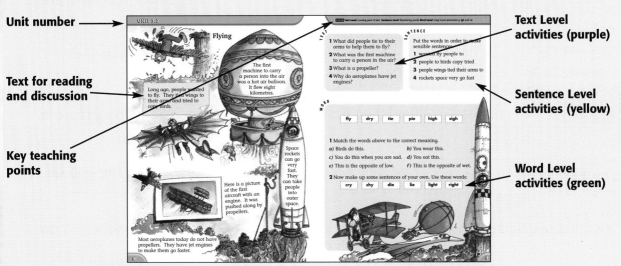

Writing Focus unit:

- appears on pages 26–29
- develops aspects of work covered in preceding ten units
- supports work on compositional writing
- contains support and suggestions for the teaching of different essential writing skills
- assumes much work will be done orally through discussion
- assumes that an adult will act as a scribe, helping children record their ideas for much of the time, and that children will only be expected to record as their developing writing competencies allow.

Phonic Check-up:

- appears on pages 30–31
- reviews the phonic work covered in the preceding ten units
- may be used to provide a review of progress or as further practice in areas of concern.

High Frequency Word List

- appears on page 32
- contains words that frequently appear in children's reading and writing
- may be used to help children to recognise these words on sight and spell them correctly
- provides an easily accessible resource for spelling and reading activities and a ready reference section.

Focus

Text Level	Sentence Level	Word Level
• Recounting main incidents in sequence	Predicting missing words	Long vowel phonemes **ee** and **ea**
• Locating parts of text	Reordering words	Long vowel phonemes **y**, **igh** and **i-e**
• Picking out incidents	Using capital letters and full stops	Long vowel phonemes **ai** and **ay**
• Locating parts of text	Using capital letters and question marks	Long vowel phoneme **i-e**
• Ordering main incidents	Expecting a text to make sense	Long vowel phoneme **a-e**
• Identifying features of poems	Using capital letters and full stops	Long vowel phonemes **oa** and **ow**
• Ordering main incidents	Predicting missing words	Long vowel phoneme **o-e**
• Characterisation	Expecting written text to make sense	Suffixing with **ing** and **ed**
• Identifying features	Using capital letters and question marks	Long vowel phonemes **oo**, **ew** and **ue**
• Picking out incidents	Predicting missing words	Long vowel phoneme **u-e**

(Year 1, Term 3)

Writing Focus	*Continuing a story; Using diagrams to write a report; Writing rhymes; Writing a story sequel; Writing a recount*
Phonic Check-up	*Review of Word Level skills covered in Units 3.1–3.10*

CONTENTS

Range	UNIT		Page
Story about fantasy worlds	**3.1**	Monkey Tricks!	6
Information text	**3.2**	Flying	8
Poem with patterned and predictable structure	**3.3**	In the Park	10
Recount of a visit	**3.4**	Our Visit to the Farm	12
Story about fantasy worlds	**3.5**	The Dragon Who Came to Breakfast	14
Poem with patterned and predictable structure	**3.6**	Imagine if…	16
Recount of a visit	**3.7**	At the Opticians	18
Story about fantasy worlds	**3.8**	The Magic Trainers	20
Poem with patterned and predictable structure	**3.9**	Shoes	22
Story about fantasy worlds	**3.10**	Dan and the Dinosaurs	24
		Writing Focus	26
		Phonic Check-up	30
		High Frequency Word List	32

Monkey Tricks!

One day Monkey, Elephant, Zebra, Hippo and Lion went for a picnic. They took some cheese rolls and set off. At the top of a steep hill they sat down. Monkey wanted all the food. He had a plan.

Monkey said to Elephant, "Have a roll." Elephant rolled over and over, right down to the bottom of the hill. Bump, bump, bump!

Then Monkey said to Zebra, "Have a roll." Zebra rolled over and over, right down to the bottom of the hill. Bump, bump, bump!

Next Monkey said to Hippo, "Why don't you have a roll?" Hippo rolled over and over, right down to the bottom of the hill as well. Bump, bump, bump!

"I think I will have a roll, too," Lion said. So Lion rolled over and over, right down to the bottom of the hill. Bump, bump, bump!

"That's better!" said Monkey. "Now all the others have gone, I can eat all the rolls myself!"

T

1 Who rolled down the hill first?

2 Who rolled down the hill second?

3 Who rolled down the hill third?

4 Who rolled down the hill last?

5 What do you think of Monkey's plan?

TENCE

Choose a sensible word to copy and complete each sentence.

1 One day the animals decided to have a _____.

2 They took some cheese _____ to eat.

3 They stopped at the top of a steep _____.

4 Monkey wanted all the _____.

5 Monkey had a _____.

D

see	eat	tree	mean	teach	need	beat
leap	weed	clean	weep	beak	feel	
cheap	speak	heel	steep	reach	green	keen

ea words	ee words
eat	tree

Draw a chart like this. Copy each word from the wall into the correct column.

7

Flying

Long ago, people wanted to fly. They tied wings to their arms and tried to copy birds.

The first machine to carry a person into the air was a hot air balloon. It flew eight kilometres.

Space rockets can go very fast. They can take people into outer space.

Here is a picture of the first aircraft with an engine. It was pushed along by propellers.

Most aeroplanes today do not have propellers. They have jet engines to make them go faster.

TEXT

1 What did people tie to their arms to help them to fly?

2 What was the first machine to carry a person in the air?

3 What is a propeller?

4 Why do aeroplanes have jet engines?

SENTENCE

Put the words in order to make sensible sentences.

1 wanted fly people to

2 people to birds copy tried

3 people wings tied their arms to

4 rockets space very go fast

WORD

| fly | dry | tie | pie | high | sigh |

1 Match the words above to the correct meaning.

a) Birds do this.

b) You wear this.

c) You do this when you are sad.

d) You eat this.

e) This is the opposite of low.

f) This is the opposite of wet.

2 Now make up some sentences of your own. Use these words:

| cry | shy | die | lie | light | right |

In the Park

I met a lion in the park,
I took him home for tea,
But when I'd fed him bread and jam,
He wouldn't play with me.

I met a camel in the rain,
We both got very wet,
But when I took him home to Mum,
He wouldn't be my pet.

I met a monkey in the street,
She had a baby, too,
But when I asked them home to lunch,
They went to Timbuctoo.

I met my daddy at the shop,
He'd bought me a surprise.
It had a little curly tail,
And big brown puppy eyes.

From First Rhymes *by Lucy Coats*

TEXT

1 What did the girl meet in the park?

2 What did the girl give the lion to eat?

3 Which animal did the girl meet in the rain?

4 What did the monkey have with her?

5 What did the girl's daddy buy her?

SENTENCE

Write these sentences again. Remember the capital letters and full stops.

1 i took the lion home for tea

2 when i met the camel it was raining

3 we both got wet in the rain

4 in the shop i saw my daddy

5 my daddy gave me a surprise

WORD

1 Choose **ai** or **ay** to complete each word.

pl__

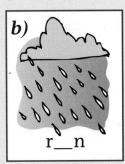

r__n

dr__n

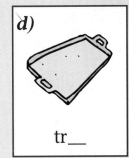

tr__

n__l

p__

cl__

p__nt

2 Use these words to complete the sentences:

| end | middle |

The letters **ai** come in the _____ of the words.
The letters **ay** come at the _____ of the words.

Our Visit to the Farm

Last week our class went on a visit to a farm.

We went by coach.

On the coach we sang songs.

When we got to the farm we saw lots of animals.

First we saw some small lambs. Their wool was white and curly.

Next we saw some baby chicks. Their feathers were yellow and fluffy.

Then we had a picnic in a big barn and sat on some straw.

The bit I liked best was when our teacher stood in a cow pat!

TEXT

1 Where did the class go?

2 What did the children see first?

3 What did the children see after the lambs?

4 Where did the children have their picnic?

5 What happened to the teacher?

SENTENCE

Write these questions again. Use capital letters and question marks correctly.

1 did the children go by coach

2 what did they do on the coach

3 were there many animals at the farm

4 did the lambs have any wool

5 what did the children sit on

WORD

1 Choose the correct word for each picture.

a)
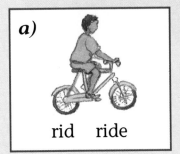
rid   ride

b)

din   dine

c)
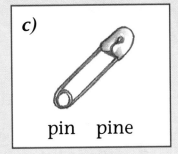
pin   pine

d)

win   wine

e)
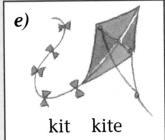
kit   kite

f)
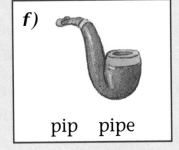
pip   pipe

2 Match up the pairs of rhyming words.

| mice | slide | bike | smile | dive |

| hide | file | nice | five | like |

13

The Dragon Who Came to Breakfast

When Ben went down for his breakfast he could hear a funny noise in the kitchen. When he opened the door... there was a DRAGON!

"Hello!" the dragon said.

"Would you like some eggs?" Ben asked.
"Yes, please!" said the dragon, and ate the lot – shells and all.

"Would you like some beans?" Ben asked.
"Yes, please!" said the dragon, and swallowed the tin in one go.

"Would you like some orange juice?" Ben asked.
"Yes, please!" said the dragon. There was a loud hiss as he swallowed.

By now the dragon was full.
"Well, I must be off. Thanks for breakfast!" said the dragon.
He got up, flapped his wings and flew off with a puff of smoke.

Ben wondered where the dragon was going for lunch.

T E X T

Put these sentences in the correct order to tell the story.

◆ The dragon drank some orange juice.

◆ The dragon ate some eggs.

◆ Ben found a dragon in the kitchen.

◆ The dragon ate a tin of beans.

◆ The dragon flew off.

S E N T E N C E

Rewrite these sentences so they make sense.

1 When Ben opened the dragon he saw a door.

2 The dragon drank some beans.

3 The dragon ate some orange juice.

4 The dragon flapped his feet and flew off.

W O R D

1 Choose the correct word for each picture.

a)

mad   made

b)
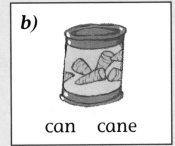
can   cane

c)
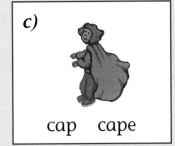
cap   cape

d)
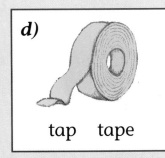
tap   tape

e)
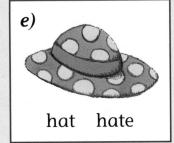
hat   hate

f)
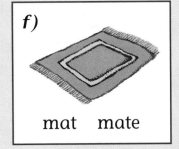
mat   mate

2 Match up the pairs of rhyming words.

cake   sale   late   gave   came

date   save   game   pale   shake

15

Imagine if...

Imagine if the sea was in the sky,

Imagine if trees grew under the ground,

Imagine if all the fish had sharp teeth,

Imagine if all the cows were round;

Imagine if all the birds flew backwards,

Imagine if a monkey was king of the land;

Imagine if bricks fell down instead of rain,

Imagine if all the seas were sand;

Imagine if everyone had seven heads,

Imagine if we all spoke Double Dutch,

Imagine if the sun came out at night –

We wouldn't like it much!

 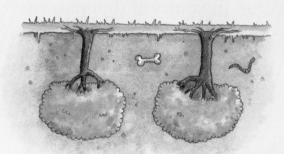

TEXT

1 What is the rhyme called?

2 Is it a silly or sensible rhyme?

3 How many lines are there in the rhyme?

4 Find the word that rhymes with:

  a) ground

  b) land

  c) Dutch

5 Do you agree with the last line?

SENTENCE

Write these sentences again. Remember the capital letters and full stops.

1 the sea is not in the sky

2 some fish have sharp teeth

3 birds cannot fly backwards

4 a person only has one head

5 the sun comes out in the day

WORD

1 Choose **oa** or **ow** to complete each word.

a)
wind__

b)
b__t

c)
r__d

d)
sn__

e)
l__f

f)
shad__

g)
thr__

h)
c__ch

2 Use these words to complete the sentences:

| end | middle |

The letters **oa** come in the _____ of the words.

The letters **ow** come at the _____ of the words.

At the Opticians

My dad took me to see the optician.
The optician asked me to read some letters on a card.
I could read the big letters at the top.
I could not read the small letters at the bottom.

The optician looked in my eyes with a little bright light.
Then she tried some different glasses on me. They helped me read the letters much better!

She helped me choose some glasses.
My dad said they looked lovely.
Now I can see everything much more clearly.
Do you like my new glasses?

TEXT

Put these sentences in the correct order to tell the story.

◆ The optician said I needed to wear glasses.

◆ I had to read some letters on a card.

◆ I went to the opticians.

◆ The optician looked in my eyes with a bright light.

◆ The optician helped me to choose some glasses.

SENTENCE

Think of a sensible word to complete each sentence.

1 My Dad took me to _____ the optician.

2 The optician _____ me to read some letters on a card.

3 The optician _____ in my eyes with a bright light.

4 She _____ me choose some frames.

WORD

1 Choose the correct word for each picture.

a)
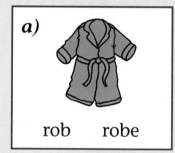
rob   robe

b)
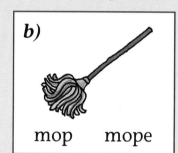
mop   mope

c)
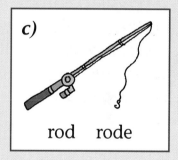
rod   rode

d)

hop   hope

e)
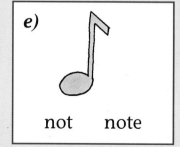
not   note

f)
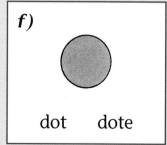
dot   dote

2 Match up the pairs of rhyming words.

pole	spoke	bone	rope	nose

broke	slope	hole	close	stone

19

The Magic Trainers

Do you wish you could fly?

One day Beth and her mum went shopping. They went into the shoe shop. Beth saw some lovely pink trainers. They were just what she wanted. Beth tried them on. They were perfect. Her mum said she could have them because her old pair were worn out. As Beth went home she felt very excited.

The first thing Beth did when she got home was to put on her new pink trainers. As she did she felt very odd. She started to float in the air and fly like a bird! The trainers were magic!

She flew up and up, high in the sky. When she looked down, everything looked smaller – the cars looked like beetles and the people looked as small as ants! Her house looked like a little box! Beth decided to fly off to see what else she could see.

TEXT

1 What was the name of the girl?

2 Where did she go with her mum?

3 What did she buy?

4 What happened when she put the trainers on?

5 What did the cars and the people look like when Beth flew in the sky?

SENTENCE

Rewrite these sentences so they are correct.

1 Beth went to the supermarket with her mum.

2 Beth bought some slippers.

3 The trainers were black.

4 When Beth put the trainers on she rode her bike.

5 The cars looked like snails.

WORD

Copy this chart. Write the new words you make.

	add **ing**	add **ed**
look	look**ing**	look**ed**
start		
open		
float		
help		
kick		
lift		
mend		
play		

21

Shoes

Red shoes, blue shoes,
Old shoes, new shoes.
Shoes that are comfy,
Shoes that are tight,
Shoes that are black,
Shoes that are white.
Shoes with buckles,
Shoes with bows,
Shoes that are narrow
And pinch your toes.
Shoes that are yellow,
Shoes that are green,
Shoes that are dirty,
Shoes that are clean.
Shoes for cold weather,
Shoes for when it's hot.
Shoes with laces
That get tangled in a knot!

Taken from Scholastic Collections – Early Years by John Foster

TEXT

1 What is the poem called?

2 Who wrote the poem?

3 How many lines are there in the poem?

4 How many different colours can you find in it?

5 Which word rhymes with:
   a) tight   *b)* bows
   c) green   *d)* hot

SENTENCE

Write these questions again. Remember the capital letters and question marks.

1 do you like red shoes

2 are narrow shoes good for you

3 when did you get your shoes

4 what shoes do you like best

5 where can you buy shoes

WORD

new	blue	food	cool	few	chew	glue
	shoot	root	true	drew	screw	soon	
clue	moon	grew	threw	hoop	roof	flew

Draw a chart like this. Write each word from the box above in the correct column.

ew words	**oo** words	**ue** words
new	food	blue

23

Dan and the Dinosaurs

One day Uncle Bob took Dan to the museum. Dan saw lots of dinosaur skeletons.

Dan saw:

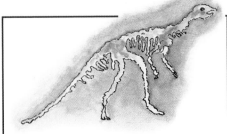

dinosaurs with long tails

flying dinosaurs

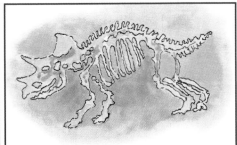

and dinosaurs with horns.

Uncle Bob said that many dinosaurs were friendly. Some were huge animals with long necks and long tails. They spent most of their time eating leaves.

Apatosaurus

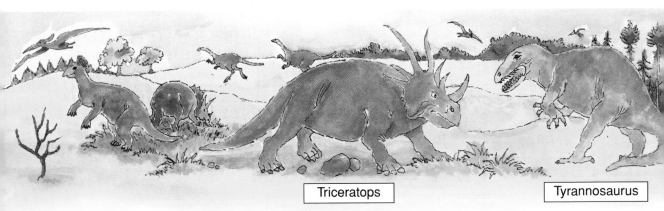

Triceratops

Tyrannosaurus

Uncle Bob said that some dinosaurs were fierce. They had sharp teeth and claws.

That night when he went to sleep, Dan dreamed about dinosaurs. In the middle of the night there was a tapping sound on his window. Dan woke up and went to have a look…

TEXT

1 Where did Uncle Bob take Dan?

2 What did the Apatosaurus eat?

3 Was the Apatosaurus a small animal?

4 Was the Tyrannosaurus friendly or fierce?

5 What do you think was tapping on Dan's window?

SENTENCE

Think of a sensible word to complete each sentence.

1 Dan saw lots of dinosaurs in the _____ .

2 The Apatosaurus had a long neck and a long _____ .

3 The Tyrannosaurus had a strong jaw and sharp _____ .

4 When Dan went to sleep, he _____ about dinosaurs.

5 In the night there was a _____ sound on his window.

WORD

1 Choose the correct word for each picture.

a)

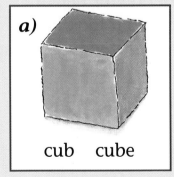

cub   cube

b)

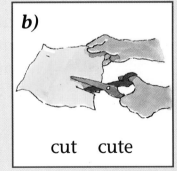

cut   cute

c)

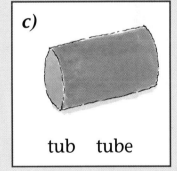

tub   tube

2 Match up the pairs of rhyming words.

cube	tune	rule	cute	use	plume

mule	fume	tube	fuse	prune	flute

25

1. Continuing a story

1 The animals get their own back!

Read Unit 3.1 again.

When the animals find out that Monkey has tricked them, they decide to get their own back on him.

◆ Write about a trick they play on him.

2 The Dinosaur in the night

Read Unit 3.10 again.

When Dan wakes up, he finds a dinosaur tapping at his window.

– Is it friendly or fierce?
– What does it look like?
– What does it want?
– What does it do?

◆ Write what happens.

2. Using diagrams to write a report

1 Read Unit 3.2 again.

Look at this diagram of a helicopter.

Read the labels.

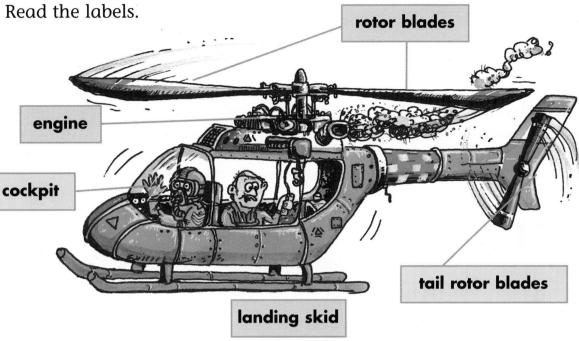

rotor blades

engine

cockpit

tail rotor blades

landing skid

◆ Use the diagram to help you match up the sentences below with the labels.

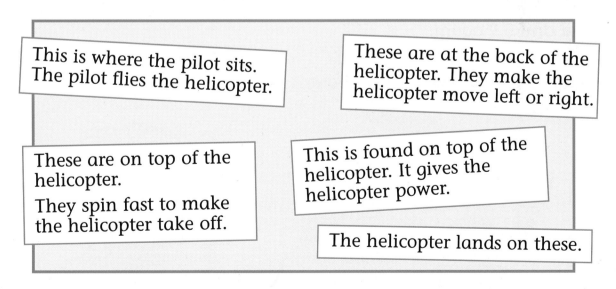

This is where the pilot sits. The pilot flies the helicopter.

These are at the back of the helicopter. They make the helicopter move left or right.

These are on top of the helicopter.

They spin fast to make the helicopter take off.

This is found on top of the helicopter. It gives the helicopter power.

The helicopter lands on these.

◆ Now write some of your own information about a helicopter.

3. Writing rhymes

1 A rhyme about animals

Read Unit 3.3 again.

◆ Make up some silly sentences about some animals *you* meet.
Do it like this:

> I met a snake, eating a cake.
> I met a crocodile, with a lovely smile.
> I met a yak, with a sack on his back.
> I met a bear, with purple hair.

2 A rhyme about clothes

Read Unit 3.9 again.
Choose an item of clothing.
◆ Make up your own rhyme about it.
Do it like this:

> T-shirts big,
> T-shirts tiny,
> T-shirts dull,
> T-shirts shiny.

4. Writing a story sequel

1 **The beast who came to breakfast**

Read Unit 3.5 again.

Imagine that one day you came down to breakfast and found a wild animal at your table.

– What would you say?

– What would you do?

◆ Write a story to tell what happens.

2 **The Magic Trainers**

Read Unit 3.8 again.

– Where else did Beth fly? Over the sea? Over a jungle? Over the desert? Over a mountain?

– What did she see?

– What did she do?

◆ Write about what happened.

5. Writing a recount

Read Units 3.4 and 3.7 again.

◆ Write about a visit you have been on.

Where did you go?
– to a museum?
– to a theme park?
– to the doctor's?
– somewhere else?

Who did you go with?
Why did you go?
What did you do?
What did you see?
What happened?

Phonic Check-up

1 Choose the correct letters to fill in each gap.

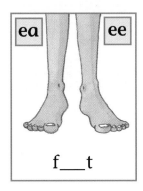 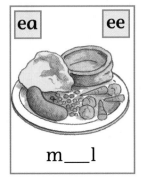  

f__t   m__l   t__cher   sl__p

2 Find and circle the words that are 'hiding'. The first has been done for you.

a) a b c f l y w   *b)* q p i e g t j   *c)* h i g h z x c

d) q w e s i g h   *e)* f g h c r y k   *f)* b t i e x n m

3 Choose the correct letters to fill in each gap.

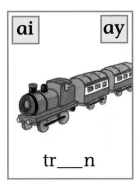 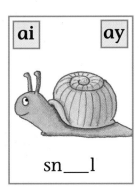 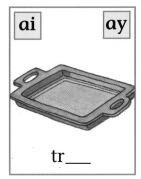 

tr__n   sn__l   tr__   h__

4 Choose the correct word to fill each gap.

a) You can prick yourself with a _____ (pin/pine).

b) Some people drink _____ (win/wine).

c) You fly a _____ (kit/kite).

d) You _____ a bike (rid/ride).

Match the words with the pictures.

wave	rope	cake	robe

Choose the correct letters to fill in each gap.

oa ow	oa ow	oa ow	oa ow
g__t	m__	t__d	bl__

Take the **ing** off each word. Write the word you are left with.

a) looking   *b)* opening   *c)* helping   *d)* lifting

Match up each word to its meaning.

a) the colour of the sky

b) not many

c) this is on top of a house

d) not old

e) an animal like a donkey

f) you stick things with this

g) you hum this

h) not hot

new

mule

cool

few

blue

tune

roof

glue

High Frequency Word list

about
after
again
an
another
as

back
ball
be
because
bed
been
boy
brother
but
by

call(ed)
came
can't
could

did
do
don't
door
down

first
from

girl
good
got

had
half
has
have
help
her
here
him

his
home
house
how

if

jump
just

last
laugh
little
live(d)
love

made
make
man
many
may
more
much
must

name
new
next
night
not
now

off
old
once
one
or
our
out
over

people
pull
push
put

ran

saw
school
seen
should
sister
so
some

take
than
that
their
them
then
there
these
three
time
too
took
tree
two

us

very

want
water
way
were
what
when
where
who
will
with
would

your